Bible Verses Cursive Handwriting Practice Writing Workbook

Marie Matthews

Bible Verses Cursive Handwriting Practice Writing Workbook

Bible Verses Cursive Handwriting Practice Writing Workbook

Marie Matthews

copyright (c) 2012

All rights are reserved.

All verses are from the King James Version of the *Bible*.

Religion > Christianity > Education > Writing

FIRST EDITION, September 2012

First printing, September 2012

ISBN-10:   1479381225

ISBN-13:   978-1479381227

INSTRUCTIONS

On each page, a Bible verse appears written in cursive in large letters across six lines.

Each page also has six blank lines. The six blank lines have the three traditional horizontal lines to help students align the top, middle, and bottom of each letter.

Copy each line of the Bible verse onto the blank line below it.

Bible Verses Cursive Handwriting Practice Writing Workbook

Verse 1   Deuteronomy 11:1

Therefore thou shalt love the Lord thy God, and keep his charge, and his statutes, and his judgments, and his commandments, alway.

Bible Verses Cursive Handwriting Practice Writing Workbook

Verse 2   Psalm 8:1

O Lord our Lord,

how excellent is thy

name in all the earth!

who hast set thy

glory above the

heavens.

Bible Verses Cursive Handwriting Practice Writing Workbook

Verse 3   Genesis 1:27

So God created man

in his own image, in

the image of God

created he him; male

and female created he

them.

Bible Verses Cursive Handwriting Practice Writing Workbook

Verse 4   Deuteronomy 4:39

Know therefore this day,

and consider it in thine

heart, that the Lord he is

God in heaven above,

and upon the earth

beneath: there is none else.

Verse 5 John 14:19

Yet a little while,

and the world seeth

me no more; but

ye see me: because

I live, ye shall live

also.

Bible Verses Cursive Handwriting Practice Writing Workbook

Verse 6   Psalm 23:6

Surely goodness and mercy shall follow me all the days of my life: and I will dwell in the house of the Lord for ever.

Bible Verses Cursive Handwriting Practice Writing Workbook

Verse 7   Ecclesiastes 4:13

Better is a poor

and a wise child

than an old and

foolish king, who

will no more be

admonished.

Bible Verses Cursive Handwriting Practice Writing Workbook

Verse 8 Genesis 2:3

And God blessed the seventh day, and sanctified it: because that in it he had rested from all his work which God created and made.

Verse 9 — Psalm 4:3

But know that the Lord

hath set apart him that

is godly for himself:

the Lord will hear

when I call unto

him.

Bible Verses Cursive Handwriting Practice Writing Workbook

Verse 10 — Romans 5:8

But God commendeth

his love toward

us, in that, while

we were yet sinners,

Christ died for

us.

Bible Verses Cursive Handwriting Practice Writing Workbook

Verse 11 　　　　　　　　　　　　　　　 John 3:16

For God so loved the

world, that he gave his

only begotten Son, that

whosoever believeth in

him should not perish,

but have everlasting life.

Verse 12 — Psalm 36:7

How excellent is thy

lovingkindness, O God!

therefore the children of

men put their trust

under the shadow of

thy wings.

Verse 13 — Mark 11:25

And when ye stand

praying, forgive, if ye

have ought against any:

that your Father also

which is in heaven may

forgive you your trespasses.

Verse 14 — John 14:6

Jesus saith unto him, I am the way, the truth, and the life: no man cometh unto the Father, but by me.

Verse 15 — Genesis 2:2

And on the seventh day

God ended his work

which he had made; and

he rested on the seventh

day from all his work

which he had made.

Bible Verses Cursive Handwriting Practice Writing Workbook

Verse 16   Psalm 147:1

Praise ye the Lord:

for it is good to

sing praises unto our

God; for it is

pleasant, and praise

is comely.

Bible Verses Cursive Handwriting Practice Writing Workbook

Verse 17 — 1 Timothy 4:12

Let no man despise thy youth; but be thou an example of the believers, in word, in conversation, in charity, in spirit, in faith, in purity.

Bible Verses Cursive Handwriting Practice Writing Workbook

Verse 18   2 Peter 3:18

But grow in grace, and

in the knowledge of

our Lord and Saviour

Jesus Christ. To him be

glory both now and

for ever. A-men.

Bible Verses Cursive Handwriting Practice Writing Workbook

Verse 19 — Romans 10:9

That if thou shalt confess

with thy mouth the Lord

Jesus, and shalt believe in

thine heart that God

hath raised him from the

dead, thou shalt be saved.

Bible Verses Cursive Handwriting Practice Writing Workbook

Verse 20   Exodus 20:7

Thou shalt not take the

name of the Lord thy

God in vain; for the

Lord will not hold him

guiltless that taketh

his name in vain.

Verse 21 — Psalm 19:8

The statutes of the Lord are right, rejoicing the heart: the commandment of the Lord is pure, enlightening the eyes.

Verse 22 — Isaiah 26:3

Thou wilt keep him

in perfect peace,

whose mind is

stayed on thee:

because he trusteth

in thee.

Verse 23 — Romans 5:1

Therefore being

justified by faith,

we have peace

with God through

our Lord Jesus

Christ.

Bible Verses Cursive Handwriting Practice Writing Workbook

Verse 24   Philippians 4:7

And the peace of

God, which passeth

all understanding,

shall keep your hearts

and minds through

Christ Jesus.

Bible Verses Cursive Handwriting Practice Writing Workbook

Verse 25 John 14:16

And I will pray

the Father, and he

shall give you another

Comforter, that he

may abide with you

for ever.

Verse 26　　　　　　　　　　　　Mark 11:26

But if ye do not

forgive, neither will

your Father which

is in heaven

forgive your

trespasses.

Verse 27 — Philippians 4:9

Those things, which ye

have both learned, and

received, and heard, and

seen in me, do: and

the God of peace shall

be with you.

Bible Verses Cursive Handwriting Practice Writing Workbook

Verse 28   Psalm 25:5

Lead me in thy

truth, and teach

me: for thou art

the God of my

salvation; on thee do

I wait all the day.

Verse 29 — Proverbs 28:13

He that covereth

his sins shall not

prosper: but whoso

confesseth and

forsaketh them shall

have mercy.

Verse 30 — Psalm 105:1

O Give thanks

unto the Lord;

call upon his name:

make known his

deeds among the

people.

Verse 31 — Ephesians 4:32

And be ye kind

one to another,

tenderhearted, forgiving

one another, even as

God for Christ's sake

hath forgiven you.

Verse 32 — Philippians 1:6

Being confident of this very thing, that he which hath begun a good work in you will perform it until the day of Jesus Christ.

Verse 33　　　　　　　　　　Ephesians 6:8

Knowing that

whatsoever good thing

any man doeth, the

same shall he receive

of the Lord, whether

he be bond or free.

Verse 34 Jude 1:24

Now unto him that is able to keep you from falling, and to present you faultless before the presence of his glory with exceeding joy.

Verse 35 — Proverbs 16:7

When a man's ways please the Lord, he maketh even his enemies to be at peace with him.

Verse 36 — Matthew 18:20

For where two or

three are gathered

together in my

name, there am I

in the midst of

them.

Verse 37 John 14:16

And I will pray the

Father, and he shall

give you another

Comforter, that he

may abide with you

for ever.

Verse 38　　　　　　　　　　　Ephesians 2:8

For by grace are

ye saved through

faith; and that

not of yourselves:

it is the gift of

God.

Verse 39   James 1:12

Blessed is the man that

endureth temptation: for

when he is tried, he shall

receive the crown of life,

which the Lord hath promised

to them that love him.

Verse 40 — James 5:15

And the prayer of faith shall save the sick, and the Lord shall raise him up; and if he have committed sins, they shall be forgiven him.

Verse 41   Matthew 6:13

And lead us not into temptation, but deliver us from evil: For thine is the kingdom, and the power, and the glory, for ever. A-men.

Bible Verses Cursive Handwriting Practice Writing Workbook

Verse 42   Psalm 37:40

And the Lord shall help them, and deliver them: he shall deliver them from the wicked, and save them, because they trust in him.

Verse 43 — John 13:34

A new commandment

I give unto you,

That ye love one another;

as I have loved you,

that ye also love one

another.

Verse 44 — Psalm 27:14

Wait on the Lord:

be of good courage,

and he shall

strengthen thine

heart: wait, I say,

on the Lord.

Verse 45   John 15: 10

If ye keep my commandments, ye shall abide in my love; even as I have kept my Father's commandments, and abide in his love.

Verse 46 — Romans 8:28

And we know that all things work together for good to them that love God, to them who are the called according to his purpose.

Verse 47 — 1 John 5:4

For whosoever is born of God overcometh the world: and this is the victory that overcometh the world, even our faith.

Verse 48 Hebrews 11:1

Now faith is

the substance

of things hoped

for, the evidence

of things not

seen.

Verse 49　　　　　　　　　　1 Corinthians 1:9

God is faithful,

by whom ye were

called unto the

fellowship of his

Son Jesus Christ

our Lord.

Verse 50 — Galatians 6:4

But let every man

prove his own work,

and then shall he

have rejoicing in

himself alone, and

not in another.

Verse 51 — Colossians 3:15

And let the peace of

God rule in your

hearts, to the which

also ye are called in

one body; and be

ye thankful.

Verse 52 — John 15:11

These things have I spoken unto you, that my joy might remain in you, and that your joy might be full.

Verse 53 — Psalm 32:8

I will instruct thee

and teach thee in

the way which thou

shalt go: I will

guide thee with mine

eye.

Verse 54 — Proverbs 14:26

In the fear of

the Lord is strong

confidence: and

his children shall

have a place of

refuge.

Verse 55 — Colossians 3:13

Forbearing one another,

and forgiving one

another, if any man

have a quarrel against

any: even as Christ

forgave you, so also do ye.

Verse 56 — Psalm 91:4

He shall cover thee

with his feathers,

and under his wings

shalt thou trust: his

truth shall be thy

shield and buckler.

Verse 57   Colossians 3:20

Children, obey

your parents in

all things: for

this is well

pleasing unto the

Lord.

Verse 58 — Psalm 91:2

I will say of

the Lord, He is

my refuge and my

fortress: my God;

in him will I

trust.

Verse 59 — Hebrews 4:16

Let us therefore come boldly unto the throne of grace, that we may obtain mercy, and find grace to help in time of need.

Verse 60 — 1 John 5:4

For whatsoever is born

of God overcometh

the world: and this is

the victory that

overcometh the world,

even our faith.

Verse 61 1 John 3:18

My little children,

let us not love

in word, neither

in tongue; but

in deed and in

truth.

Verse 62 — 1 John 4:4

Ye are of God, little children, and have overcome them: because greater is he that is in you, than he that is in the world.

Bible Verses Cursive Handwriting Practice Writing Workbook

Verse 63 — Matthew 7:7

Ask, and it shall

be given you; seek,

and ye shall find;

knock, and it shall

be opened unto

you.

Verse 64　　　　　　　　　　　　　　　　　Matthew 7:8

For every one that

asketh receiveth; and

he that seeketh findeth;

and to him that

knocketh it shall be

opened.

Verse 65 — Proverbs 28:7

Whoso keepeth the

law is a wise son:

but he that is a

companion of

riotous men shameth

his father.

Verse 66　　　　　　　　　　　Psalm 86:5

For thou, Lord, art good, and ready to forgive; and plenteous in mercy unto all them that call upon thee.

Bible Verses Cursive Handwriting Practice Writing Workbook

Verse 67 Matthew 2:1

Now when Jesus was

born in Bethlehem of

Judaea in the days of

Herod the King, behold,

there came wise men

from the east to Jerusalem.

Bible Verses Cursive Handwriting Practice Writing Workbook

Verse 68   Psalm 86:7

In the day of

my trouble I

will call upon

thee: for thou

wilt answer

me.

Verse 69 — John 15:7

If ye abide in me, and my words abide in you, ye shall ask what ye will, and it shall be done unto you.

Verse 70   Ephesians 6:8

Knowing that

whatsoever good thing

any man doeth, the

same shall he receive

of the Lord, whether

he be bond or free.

Verse 71 — John 14:13

And whatsoever

ye shall ask in my

name, that will I

do, that the Father

may be glorified in

the Son.

Bible Verses Cursive Handwriting Practice Writing Workbook

Verse 72   Ecclesiastes 12:13

Let us hear the conclusion of the whole matter: Fear God, and keep his commandments: for this is the whole duty of man.

Verse 73　　　　　　　　　　　　Psalm 10:17

Lord, thou hast heard the desire of the humble: thou wilt prepare their heart, thou wilt cause thine ear to hear.

Verse 74 — James 5:16

Confess your faults one to another, and pray one for another, that ye may be healed. The effectual fervent prayer of a righteous man availeth much.

Verse 75 Psalm 18:3

I will call upon

the Lord, who is

worthy to be

praised: so shall I

be saved from mine

enemies.

Verse 76 — Psalm 111:10

The fear of the Lord is the beginning of wisdom: a good understanding have all they that do his commandments: his praise endureth for ever.

Verse 77　　　　　　　　Romans 10:17 and 1 Peter 5:7

So then faith cometh

by hearing, and hearing

by the word of God.

Casting all your care

upon him; for he

careth for you.

Bible Verses Cursive Handwriting Practice Writing Workbook

Verse 78 — Romans 12:10

Be kindly affectioned

one to another

with brotherly

love; in honour

preferring one

another.

Verse 79 — 2 Corinthians 13:14

The grace of the Lord

Jesus Christ, and the

love of God, and the

communion of the

Holy Ghost, be with

you all. A-men.

Verse 80   2 Timothy 1:7

For God hath not given us the spirit of fear; but of power, and of love, and of a sound mind.

Verse 81 — Psalm 41:1

Blessed is he that considereth the poor: the Lord will deliver him in time of trouble.

Bible Verses Cursive Handwriting Practice Writing Workbook

Verse 82 — Proverbs 22:6

Train up a child

in the way he

should go: and

when he is old,

he will not depart

from it.

Verse 83 — Matthew 7:12

Therefore all things

whatsoever ye would

that men should do to

you, do ye even so to

them: for this is the

law and the prophets.

Bible Verses Cursive Handwriting Practice Writing Workbook

Verse 84   Proverbs 20:11

Even a child is

known by his

doings, whether his

work be pure, and

whether it be

right.

Verse 85 — Psalm 55:22

Cast thy burden upon the Lord, and he shall sustain thee: he shall never suffer the righteous to be moved.

Verse 86　　　　　　　　　　Psalm 98:1

O sing unto the Lord a new song; for he hath done marvellous things: his right hand, and his holy arm, hath gotten him the victory.

Verse 87 — Proverbs 19:21

There are many

devices in a man's

heart: nevertheless

the counsel of

the Lord, that shall

stand.

Verse 88   Psalm 41:2

The Lord will preserve him, and keep him alive; and he shall be blessed upon the earth: and thou wilt not deliver him unto the will of his enemies.

Verse 89 — Psalm 95:1

O come, let us

sing unto the Lord:

let us make a

joyful noise to

the rock of our

salvation.

Verse 90 — Psalm 37:5

Commit thy way

unto the Lord;

trust also in

him; and he

shall bring it

to pass.

Verse 91 — Matthew 26:41

Watch and pray,

that ye enter not

into temptation:

the spirit indeed is

willing, but the flesh

is weak.

Verse 92 — Mark 10:15

Verily I say unto

you, Whosoever shall

not receive the kingdom

of God as a little

child, he shall not

enter therein.

Verse 93 — 1 John 4:7

Beloved, let us love

one another: for love

is of God; and every

one that loveth is

born of God, and

knoweth God.

Verse 94 — 1 Corinthians 11:2

Now I praise you,

brethren, that ye

remember me in all

things, and keep the

ordinances, as I

delivered them to you.

Verse 95   1 John 4:12

No man hath seen

God at any time. If

we love one another,

God dwelleth in us,

and his love is

perfected in us.

Verse 96 — Proverbs 8:32

Now therefore

hearken unto me,

O ye children: for

blessed are they

that keep my

ways.

Bible Verses Cursive Handwriting Practice Writing Workbook

Verse 97 Psalm 112:1

Praise ye the Lord.

Blessed is the man

that feareth the Lord,

that delighteth

greatly in his

commandments.

Verse 98 — Proverbs 6:20 and 21

My son, keep thy father's commandment, and forsake not the law of thy mother: Bind them continually upon thine heart, and tie them about thy neck.

Verse 99 — Deuteronomy 6:5

And thou shalt love the Lord thy God with all thine heart, and with all thy soul, and with all thy might.

Verse 100 — Psalm 16:8

I have set the Lord

always before me:

because he is at

my right hand,

I shall not be

moved.

Verse 101 — Proverbs 3:5 and 6

Trust in the Lord with all thine heart; and lean not unto thine own understanding. In all thy ways acknowledge him, and he shall direct thy paths.

Verse 102 — Proverbs 13:20

He that walketh

with wise men

shall be wise:

but a companion

of fools shall be

destroyed.

Verse 103　　　　　　　　　　　　Isaiah 44:3

For I will pour water upon

him that is thirsty, and

floods upon the dry ground:

I will pour my spirit upon

thy seed, and my blessing

upon thine offspring.

Verse 104   Psalm 29:2

Give unto the

Lord the glory

due unto his name;

worship the Lord

in the beauty of

holiness.

Bible Verses Cursive Handwriting Practice Writing Workbook

Verse 105 　　　　　　　　　　　　　　　　　Nahum 1:7

The Lord is good,

a strong hold in

the day of trouble;

and he knoweth

them that trust

in him.

Verse 106 Isaiah 38:19

The living, the living,

he shall praise thee,

as I do this day:

the father to the

children shall make

known thy truth.

Verse 107 Isaiah 54:13

And all thy children

shall be taught of

the Lord; and

great shall be the

peace of thy

children.

Verse 108 — Luke 6:31

And as ye would that men should do to you, do ye also to them likewise.

Verse 109 — Exodus 20:12

Honour thy father

and thy mother

that thy days may

be long upon the land

which the Lord thy

God giveth thee.

Bible Verses Cursive Handwriting Practice Writing Workbook

Verse 110   Hebrews 13:18

Pray for us; for

we trust we have

a good conscience,

in all things

willing to live

honestly.

Verse 111 — Psalm 7:1

O Lord my God,

in thee do I put

my trust: save me

from all them that

persecute me, and

deliver me.

Verse 112 　　　　　　　　　　　　Psalm 54:1 and 2

Save me, O God, by

thy name, and judge

me by thy strength.

Hear my prayer, O

God; give ear to the

words of my mouth.

Verse 113   Psalm 138:1

I will praise

thee with my

whole heart:

before the gods

will I sing praise

unto thee.

Verse 114 — Matthew 5:16

Let your light so

shine before men, that

they may see your good

works, and glorify

your Father which

is in heaven.

Verse 115 — Psalm 105:1

O Give thanks

unto the Lord;

call upon his name:

make known his

deeds among the

people.

Verse 116 — Psalm 106:1

Praise ye the Lord,

O give thanks

unto the Lord;

for he is good:

for his mercy

endureth for ever.

Bible Verses Cursive Handwriting Practice Writing Workbook

Verse 117 — Psalm 75:1

Unto thee, O God, do

we give thanks, unto

thee do we give thanks:

for that thy name is

near thy wondrous

works declare.

Bible Verses Cursive Handwriting Practice Writing Workbook

Verse 118   Psalm 48:1

Great is the Lord,

and greatly to be

praised in the city

of our God,

in the mountain

of his holiness.

Verse 119 — Psalm 59:1

Deliver me from

mine enemies,

O my God:

defend me from

them that rise up

against me.

Verse 120   1 Corinthians 15:2

By which also ye

are saved, if ye keep

in memory what I

preached unto you,

unless ye have

believed in vain.

Verse 121 — Psalm 25:1 and 2

Unto thee, O Lord, do I

lift up my soul. O my

God, I trust in thee:

let me not be ashamed,

let not mine enemies

triumph over me.

Verse 122　　　　　　　　　　1 Corinthians 15:57

But thanks be

to God, which

giveth us the

victory through

our Lord Jesus

Christ.

Bible Verses Cursive Handwriting Practice Writing Workbook

Verse 123											Psalm 34:1

I will bless

the Lord at

all times: his

praise shall

continually be

in my mouth.

Verse 124　　　　　　　　　Psalm 66:1 and 2

Make a joyful noise

unto God, all ye

lands: Sing forth

the honour of his

name: make his

praise glorious.

Verse 125 — 1 John 1:5

This then is the message

which we have heard

of him, and declare

unto you, that God is

light, and in him is

no darkness at all.

Bible Verses Cursive Handwriting Practice Writing Workbook

Verse 126   Genesis 1:16

And God made two

great lights; the greater

light to rule the day,

and the lesser light

to rule the night:

he made the stars also.

Verse 127 — 1 John 2:5

But whoso keepeth

his word, in him

verily is the love

of God perfected:

hereby know we

that we are in him.

Made in the USA
San Bernardino, CA
04 September 2017